TRACKING
DINOSAURS
IN THE
GOBI

TRACKING
DINOSAURS
IN THE
GOBI

MARGERY FACKLAM

Twenty-First Century Books
A Division of Henry Holt and Company ▸ New York

Twenty-First Century Books
A Division of Henry Holt and Company, Inc.
115 West 18th Street
New York, NY 10011

Henry Holt® and colophon are trademarks of
Henry Holt and Company, Inc.
Publishers since 1866

Published in Canada by Fitzhenry & Whiteside Ltd.
195 Allstate Parkway, Markham, Ontario, L3R 4T8

Library of Congress Cataloging-in-Publication Data
Facklam, Margery.
Tracking dinosaurs in the Gobi / Margery Facklam.
p.   cm.
Includes bibliographical references (p.) and index.
Summary: Describes the work of paleontologists, beginning with
Roy Chapman Andrews in the 1920s, who have searched in the
Gobi Desert for evidence of dinosaurs.
1. Dinosaurs—Gobi Desert (Mongolia and China)—Juvenile literature.
[1. Paleontology.   2. Paleontologists.   3. Gobi Desert (Mongolia and China).
4. Fossils.   5. Dinosaurs.]   I. Title.
QE862.D5F725 1997   97-8070
567.9'995173—dc21   CIP
                                                                   AC

ISBN 0-8050-5165-1
First Edition—1997

DESIGNED BY KELLY SOONG
MAP BY JEFFREY L. WARD

Printed in Mexico
All first editions are printed on acid-free paper ∞.
1   3   5   7   9   10   8   6   4   2

Photo Credits

Cover photo: © 1997 Louis Psihoyos/Matrix International, Inc.

pp. 2, 53, 54: © Fred Conrad; pp. 10, 33, 48, 49: © Nancy Ross Facklam; pp. 12, 34 (bottom): © UPI/Corbis-Bettmann; p. 13: © Lois Lammerhuber/Gamma Liaison; p. 16: © Culver Pictures; p. 19: Reprinted with permission of Chrysler Historical Foundation; p. 21: © AP/Wide World Photos; pp. 29, 51, 56, 63, 65, 67: Louis Psihoyos/Matrix International, Inc.; p. 32: © David G. Chardavoyne; p. 42 (inset): John Hubbard/Colgate University; p. 44 (top): © Jen & Des Bartlett/Oxford Scientific Films/Animals Animals; p. 44 (bottom): Steven David Miller/Animals Animals; p. 58: © Philippe Plailly/Eurelios/SPL/Photo Researchers, Inc.; p. 68: © Francois Gohier/Photo Researchers, Inc.

Following pages all Courtesy of Dept. of Library Services, American Museum of Natural History—p. 23: neg no. 108694; p. 24: neg. no. 251574, photo by R.C.A.; p. 31: neg. no. 251502, photo by Shackelford; p. 34 (top): transp. no. K17236; p. 39: neg. no. 410764, photo by Shackelford; p. 41: neg. no. 251630, photo by R.C.A.; p. 42: neg. no. 310548, photo by Kirschner; p. 46: neg. no. 410955, photo by Shackelford.

Author's Note

As a kid, I had read the books of Roy Chapman Andrews and longed to look for dinosaurs in the Gobi Desert. I finally had a wonderful taste of it in the summer of 1995. With my daughter-in-law, Nancy Facklam, who took some of the photographs in this book, we followed the trail of Roy Chapman Andrews from Beijing to the Gobi Desert with a small group that had been organized by the American Museum of Natural History. At the Flaming Cliffs, Michael Novacek, Mark Norell, Jim Clark, Amy Davidson, and other members of that summer's team enthusiastically led us up and down the red hills and gullies, showing us where Andrews had camped and where the famous dinosaur eggs were found.

I appreciate David Chardavoyne's generosity in helping me solve a problem with this book.

Margery Facklam

This book is dedicated to my wonderful family,
especially my husband, Howard,
who so graciously tended to things at home
while I went off to the Gobi Desert.

CONTENTS

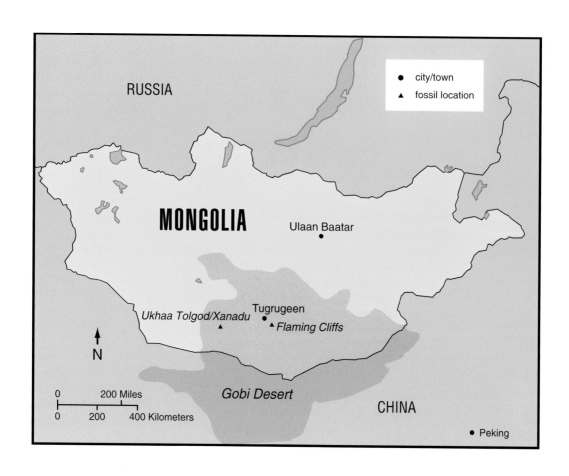

1

UNDER A LUCKY STAR

The Gobi Desert was sun-scorched after a year with no rain. The sparse, scrubby plants had shriveled, and only a few tiny, brown lizards darted into the searing sunlight to find insects. Bleached skeletons of sheep and camels lay scattered over the desolate badlands. On an April morning in 1923, clouds of dust swirled behind five Dodge touring cars and two Fulton trucks that jolted and bumped over the rutted tracks they had left the year before. A great cheer went up when the men of the Central Asiatic Expedition at last saw the red sandstone canyon they had named the Flaming Cliffs.

The next morning at sunrise, the scientists scattered over the red basin carrying brushes, small picks, and collecting sacks. In a quick search of this site at the end of the 1922 season, they had found only a few teeth, some broken eggshells, and the skull of a small reptile.

But this time, when they straggled back into camp for lunch, one of the fossil-hunters announced, "I found dinosaur eggs." The others laughed. What a great joke—dinosaur eggs! Nobody even knew for certain if dinosaurs laid eggs, but the men were curious enough to follow him to a sandstone ledge. There the kidding stopped when they saw a circle of fossil eggs, shaped like

The Flaming Cliffs, Gobi Desert, Mongolia

small loaves of French bread, embedded in the red rock. It was a discovery that would bring fame to the expedition and especially to its leader, Roy Chapman Andrews.

Mongolia's Gobi Desert is a half-million square miles of badlands, sand dunes, and canyons, where temperatures soar to 110 degrees F in summer and plunge to 50 below zero in winter. But since Andrews' expeditions, it has become the place fossil-hunters dream of exploring the way astronauts dream of going to Mars.

Explorers and adventurers had star status in the early 1900s, and Roy Chapman Andrews was one of the headliners. Some say he was the model for the Indiana Jones character. He was handsome enough to look the part, and he had enough close calls for any action movie script. If reporters at the time knew about Andrews' years as a spy for Naval Intelligence in Asia during World War I, they didn't write much about it. But they never grew tired of describing his battles against bandits, blasting sandstorms, and Chinese war-lords. However, Andrews wasn't just another daring adventurer. He was an established scientist with a superb ability for organization.

"I wanted to be an explorer and naturalist so passionately that anything else as a life work just never entered my mind," Andrews once wrote. "Of course I didn't know how I was going to do it, but I never let ways and means clutter my youthful dreams."[1]

Andrews liked to say that he was born under a lucky star, but he was the kind of man who often made his own luck. He was quick to recognize an opportunity, and he liked nothing better than to take action. Born and raised in the rural town of Beloit, Wisconsin, he was like most small-town boys who liked to hunt and fish. He said that all his life it was torture for him to stay indoors.

Andrews taught himself taxidermy. He practiced on the birds and small mammals he shot, but he became so skilled that hunters from fifty miles around brought him their game to mount. By the time he finished high school, Andrews had saved enough money from his taxidermy work to go to Beloit College. He admitted later that he hadn't been much of a student either in high school or college because he had so many other interests, but he knew what he wanted to do—work in a museum and explore. Years later, when his explorations had come to an end and he was director of the American Museum of Natural History, he loved to tell how it all began.

Before he graduated from college in 1906 he had written to sixty museums to ask for a job, but there were no offers. The director of the American

This photo shows
Roy Chapman Andrews (1884–1960)
in 1931, just a year after his last
expedition to the Gobi.

Museum of Natural History in New York City, his first choice, had also turned him down, but he said that he'd be happy to see Andrews if he was ever in New York on other business. Andrews read that as an invitation.

A few days after graduation, Andrews took the $30 he had saved and a shoe box packed with lunch for two days, and boarded the train to New York. He had never been away from Beloit, except for one ninety-mile trip to Chicago, and he was nervous about being in a big city. But when he walked out of Grand Central Station and saw New York, all his fears vanished. "It was my city," he said.

In his office at the museum, the director, Dr. H. C. Bumpus, again told Andrews that there wasn't a position of any kind open. Andrews blurted out, "I'm not asking for a position. I just want to *work* here. You have to have someone to clean the floors. Couldn't I do that?"

"But a man with a college education doesn't want to clean floors!" Dr. Bumpus said.

"No," Andrews told him, "not just *any* floors. But the museum floors are different. I'll clean them and love it, if you'll let me."[2]

And that's what happened. Andrews went to work in the taxidermy department as assistant to twenty-two-year-old James L. Clark, who later became famous as an artist of sculpture-taxidermy. Andrews mopped floors and mixed clay for the sculptures over which they stretched the animal skins. Now and then Dr. Bumpus sent for Andrews to write labels or do odd jobs. He also inspected the floors "to see if the college diploma had got in the way of the mop."[3]

A taxidermist is skilled in preparing and stuffing the skins of animals and birds.
This taxidermist is surrounded by some of his finished work.

Andrews had been at the museum only a few months when he and Clark were assigned to help build a life–size model of a whale to hang in the third-floor gallery. "What I knew about whales was less than nothing," Andrews admitted. "I had never met a whale in Wisconsin's Rock River!" But he believed that if he kept his mouth shut and his ears and eyes open, no one would know how ignorant he was.[4]

The project was a mess. The attempt to cover seventy-six feet of metal and wood framework with paper ended with a whale so misshapen that it looked like it had starved to death. Dr. Bumpus was not pleased. When he asked Andrews and Clark what *they* would do, they told him to fire the man in charge and let them finish making the whale with wire netting and papier-mâché.

It took them eight months to get the job done with a crew of helpers. Their model of the gigantic whale has since been seen by millions of museum visitors. And then Andrews' lucky star took charge again. A real whale beached and died on the coast of Long Island. Dr. Bumpus sent Andrews and Clark to "get the whole thing; photographs, measurements, baleen and skeleton—every bone!" Andrews could hardly believe it—only seven months at the museum and he was off on his first expedition.[5]

It was a staggering job. Bitter winds lashed the shore and buried the whale's bones deep in the sand. For days, the two men fought to stay on their feet in the pounding waves. With their arms in freezing water, they groped blindly with knives to cut the bones from the rotting flesh. But they got every bone, even three small rudimentary pelvic bones they rescued from a pot of melting blubber.

Very little was known about the life of whales in 1908, except from the point of view of whalers, whose only interest was in killing the great animals. When Andrews wrote his first scientific paper describing that beached whale, it launched him on what he called an eight-year career of blubber and brine that took him twice around the world. He signed on to a ship with the Pacific Whaling Company and learned more about whales than anyone had ever known, even though he was miserably seasick every day.

He wrote ". . . nothing I have ever done required more unadulterated guts than going out on those tossing, twisting whaling vessels."[6] Often he was so weak that he lay on deck like a dead body until a sailor would lift him to his feet and hold him steady enough to take notes and photographs. But he was the first naturalist to witness and describe the birth of a baby whale.

During those whaling expeditions, Andrews had his first view of Asia.

"Almost from the moment I set foot on shore at Yokohama," he wrote, "I felt that I belonged in the Orient."[7]

In eight years, Andrews became the world's leading authority on whales. Most scientists would have been satisfied to stay with a field in which they'd found success, but Andrews had the mark of an explorer—an insatiable curiosity to try something new. Not only was he hungry for the Orient, but he wanted to test a controversial theory that Asia, and not Africa, would turn out to be the birthplace of the first humans and much of the animal life of Europe and America.

Andrews said that Central Asia was a forbidding place and virtually unknown. First, he had to find out where to go and learn the customs, methods of travel, and the language. During his whaling travels, Andrews had learned to speak Japanese fluently and some Korean, but he knew that Chinese would be most useful for the expeditions he had in mind.

In 1915, Andrews presented his plan to the museum's president, Dr. Henry Fairfield Osborn, for a ten-year series of expeditions to Asia. He wanted to focus the first trip on zoology and the collection of specimens of animals from southwest China and the borders of Tibet. Osborn was delighted because he was a defender of the theory that Asia was the birthplace of mankind.

In 1914, Andrews had married Yvette Borup, the sister of an explorer friend, George Borup. She not only loved to travel and explore new lands, but she was also a skilled photographer. They sailed for China in March 1916. Over the next few years they wandered on horseback through China and Outer Mongolia, collecting mammals, birds, reptiles, fish, and insects for the museum's Asia exhibit. Yvette took hundreds of photographs. They slept on the ground in fur-lined sleeping bags, shot game for food, and bathed in streams. But Andrews felt right at home.

He later wrote, "In the painted desert of the Gobi; in steaming Borneo jungles; among palm trees on the enchanted islands of the East Indies; in the wilderness of Korean forests; on the summit of the Himalaya; along the fogbound shores of Bering Sea—wherever I made my campfire, there was 'home.'"[8]

Mongolia is halfway around the world from New York City. It extends a thousand miles from Siberia in the north, to China in the south, and two thousand miles from east to west. This sparsely populated country reminded Andrews of the prairies, plains, peaks, and clear skies of America's western states. It is a land of nomads, once ruled by the infamous Genghis Khan and his grandson Kublai Khan. Seven hundred fifty years ago the Mongols con-

Roy Chapman Andrews
and his first wife, Yvette

quered all the territory from the Pacific Ocean to Europe, with troops so skilled in horsemanship that they could sleep in their saddles and cover distances no others could manage.

Andrews wrote, "I had found my country. The one I had been born to know and love. Somewhere in the depths of the vast, silent desert lay those records of the past that I had come to seek."[9]

He knew he'd be back.

2

BIG PLANS

Before Andrews ventured into Mongolia, the only fossil ever found there was a tooth of an ancient rhinoceros picked up by a Russian geologist in 1892. Most scientists believed that the tooth had probably been found somewhere else and dropped by a passing caravan. They told Andrews that he was foolish to think of finding ancient bones in the Gobi Desert. "You might as well look for them in the ocean," one said. But Andrews had seen the digs in China where anthropologists were looking for early humans. And he knew how much the Chinese people valued the healing powers of ground-up bones of ancient animals, which they called "dragon bones." If they could be found in China, why not Mongolia?

Then when people heard that Andrews was going to use cars, they told him he really was crazy. Cars in the 1920s were far from today's all-terrain four-wheel-drive vehicles, and the only roads in Mongolia were rough, camel caravan trails. There would be more than enough problems with bandits and extremes of weather without the added trouble of cars breaking down in the middle of nowhere.

Andrews had to have the courage of his convictions to use cars in the desert. No one else thought it could be done. Many predicted that if the expedition ever returned, it would be on camels.

Camels had always been the most reliable transportation in a desert, but a camel can travel only fifteen miles a day, less if it is carrying a heavy load. With cars, the expedition could cover a hundred miles a day. Travel time in the Gobi is limited to a few months in summer, between the sudden snowstorms that can strike in late spring and early fall.

> ▶ ▶ ▶ ▶ ▶ ▶
>
> ### DRAGON BONES
>
> In some cultures, a dragon is a symbol of evil, but in China a dragon is a kindly spirit, admired for its strength and wisdom. For centuries, Chinese people have used "dragon bones" to communicate with the spirits of their honorable ancestors. Andrews suspected that some of these dragon bones might be the fossil bones of dinosaurs.

Andrews was convinced that with cars, his expedition would be able to explore more territory in one season than others did in ten.

Andrews promised museum officials that no one had tried to search the Gobi as he planned to do it. Not only would he take the best scientists in every field, but he would arrange supplies so that three or four separate, fully equipped groups could work away from the main camp for at least two weeks at a time.

Imagine organizing a camping trip to a desert so remote that you would have no way of getting help and no contact with anyone except a few nomads. There would be no phones, faxes, newspapers, letters, or telegrams, nothing but one radio receiver for a weekly time signal that would allow you to fix your longitude and latitude.

Imagine trying to think of everything you'd need for months in a desert—food, water, clothing, medical supplies, tools, cooking equipment, tents and bedding, gas, oil, and spare parts for cars. But Roy Chapman Andrews was good at this kind of planning. The difficult part would be paying for it. He thought he'd need about $250,000. That wouldn't take a big expedition very far today, but it was a lot of money in 1920, when the average American income was only $1,400 a year. The museum gave Andrews $5,000 and the America–Asiatic Association gave him $30,000, but he had to raise the rest.

The Arctic explorer Robert Peary warned Andrews that the most exhausting part of any expedition was raising the money, and Andrews found out how true that was. With slides from Yvette's photographs of their travels and his own enthusiasm, Andrews raised $200,000 from New York's wealthiest

This 1920 Dodge touring car is similar to those
Andrews took on his first expedition into the Gobi.

people. He said he spoke at so many dinners and luncheons, lectured before so many audiences, interviewed so many financiers, and wrote so much about the Central Asiatic Expedition that it had become a nightmare.

When Andrews held a press conference to invite public support to raise the rest of the money, he was surprised that newspapers focused on the idea of finding prehistoric humans rather than on the broad scope of these explorations. Front-page headlines called it THE MISSING LINK EXPEDITION, which stirred up controversy over evolution.

Despite that, thousands of letters and telegrams arrived at the museum, most with donations, but many asking to join the expedition. A thousand letters were from women, including one who offered to bring along her ouija board to help find the Missing Link. A waiter, who said he had his own tuxedo, wanted to serve the meals, and a butcher offered to be Andrews' bodyguard. An artist, ex-army men, and many young boys and girls longing for adventure begged to go along.

Several friends who played polo with Andrews said they'd pay their own way, but Andrews turned them down, too. The expedition was serious scientific business, not a game. He also turned down money from an oil company and a mining syndicate because the governments of China and Mongolia were suspicious that Americans were only looking for precious natural resources.

Choosing the staff was the part Andrews liked best. He knew exactly the kind of men he wanted with him—not only the best scientists, but also men who were loyal and dedicated to the job. Andrews' first choice was Walter Granger. As the expedition's second in command, Granger was actually the scientific leader. Like Andrews, Granger had started work at the American Museum of Natural History in the taxidermy department, but he had become an expert paleontologist with years of experience in the field.

Andrews also hired geologists, an archaeologist, a botanist, a zoologist, a motor chief, mechanics, surveyors, mapmakers, taxidermists, and a photographer.

Knowing they'd need a year to get ready, Granger and Andrews, with their wives and a few other expedition members, went on ahead of the others to set up headquarters in 1921. When they arrived in China's capital, Peking (Beijing), thick swirls of choking, yellow dust howled through the city. It was the worst dust storm in twenty years. One Chinese official warned them that it was an omen of famine, war, disease, and death because the gods were against them.

Andrews and his crew moved into an enormous, sprawling summer home they had rented as their headquarters at the edge of the Forbidden City, an area of the capital that includes palaces of former Chinese emperors. More than a hundred small rooms that surrounded the courtyards were remodeled into forty-seven larger rooms for comfortable living quarters, bathrooms, a photo lab, garages, stables, and a motion picture studio. Inside its tiled and gated walls, the compound gradually became the staging area for a major expedition. Meanwhile, Andrews lived in luxury, waited on by dozens of servants. He played polo, went hunting, and partied with ambassadors and other foreigners living in Peking.

But he also tended to the business of gathering supplies for the expedition. Like other explorers, Andrews knew that the natives of any country developed the best clothing and housing for survival in their land, so he bought Mongolian sheepskin-lined sleeping bags and fur-lined coats and hats for every expedition member. He also bought the native blue cotton tents designed to stand against the fierce winds that whipped across the desert.

Andrews hired a staff of Chinese and Mongolian men as cooks, drivers, interpreters, and guides. He was especially satisfied with his choice of a Mongolian named Merin to lead the caravan. (Mongolians traditionally use

While Andrews was at his headquarters in Peking (Beijing),
he visited the emperor in his luxurious Summer Palace, shown here.

only one name.) Merin knew camels and the desert better than anyone, and he was as reliable as the rising sun. More than once, Merin would appear at the head of the caravan on his white camel—the American flag flying from the saddle—at the appointed place in the desert, on the agreed-upon date, to meet the motorized unit, sometimes after weeks of extreme hardships.

In his journal that summer, Andrews wrote: "Mongolian camels should graze all summer, storing up fat so their humps will carry them through the winter months when food is scarce. We had to reverse the procedure by working them in the summer."[1]

For carrying supplies, including two tons of flour, thousands of pounds of rice, dried fruits and vegetables, and other staples, Andrews ordered wooden boxes made with sliding tops. As the boxes were emptied, they became the crates for shipping fossils back to Peking and on to America. Each of the seventy-five camels on that first expedition carried four hundred pounds of supplies in these boxes. Each camel also carried forty gallons of gas and about a gallon of oil stored in metal cans.

When people asked him about the hardships, Andrews had a quick reply—"Personally, I do not believe in hardships." But then he added, "Sleeping on the ground and eating the simplest food isn't a hardship for me. If you want to do something badly enough there will be few hardships in it. If you don't want to do it, everything will be a hardship."[2]

Andrews apparently didn't think it was a hardship to be cut off from all communication. Now and then a caravan might deliver cablegrams and mail to them out in the field, but Andrews had decided that they would be better off without two-way radio communication. If they heard bad news from home—family illness or death, for example—there was nothing they could do about it. There was no way to get home quickly, and they'd be depressed and distracted from work.

One night a week, at ten minutes to ten, the group gathered around the radio receiver to listen for the dots and dashes from an operator at the U.S. Navy base in the Philippine Islands. "Here goes for those fellows up in the Gobi Desert," the message said, followed by the precise time signal.

Andrews wondered if the operator in the tropics ever tried to picture the long semicircle of blue tents in the desert, the restless camels, and the men muffled in fur-lined coats huddled around the receiver.

One of his pet peeves had to do with adventure, which seems strange coming from a man whose whole life appeared to be one long adventure. He liked to quote the polar explorer Vilhjalmur Stefansson, who said, "Adventures are

In this group photo of members of the expedition, cooks are in the top row, staff is in the middle row, and interpreters and camel drivers are in the bottom row.

a mark of incompetence." To that Andrews would add, "Adventures are a nuisance. They interfere with work."[3]

What he meant, of course, was that adventures are often the result of mistakes—carelessness or bad planning. In fifteen years, he remembered "just" ten times where he had really narrow escapes from death—two from near-drownings in typhoons; one when a boat was charged by a wounded whale; once when he and his wife were nearly eaten by starving dogs; once when he

Camels were an important part of Andrews' expeditions into
the Gobi, for often they could go where cars could not.
Even today, camels carry people and goods in Mongolia.

was threatened by fanatical lama priests; two close calls when he fell over cliffs; once when he was nearly caught by a huge python (he hated snakes); and twice when he was almost killed by bandits.

Whenever Andrews started on an expedition, his insurance company canceled his accident policy. Not even Lloyd's of London would insure him, and that company is known for insuring just about anything.

On the other hand, Andrews admitted that every expedition member had to be ready to handle whatever came along—cars sunk hub-deep in slimy mud, sudden blinding sandstorms that tore the shirts from their backs, or thirst so bad that their tongues swelled out of their mouths. But during all the years of the expedition, with from thirty-five to forty men in the field, they had no serious accidents, although Andrews did shoot himself in the leg once.

On April 17, 1922, the first of the Central Asiatic Expeditions was ready to move out. Andrews, the other scientists, and Yvette, who traveled with them the first few weeks before returning to Peking, piled into five Dodge touring cars. Followed by two trucks loaded with equipment, they roared through the gateway of the Great Wall of China, north to Mongolia.

Five weeks earlier, a caravan of seventy-five Bactrian camels led by Merin on his white camel had set out in single file with orders to meet the expedition at an oasis six hundred miles out in the desert. At designated spots along the way, the caravan would leave gas, oil, water, and food supplies.

The 1922 expedition was planned as a reconnaissance mission. In his daily journal Andrews wrote, ". . . war and changing politics, bandits, and the peril of the trail make it a gambler's chance—big risk for big gain—everything on the turn of a card."[4]

But by the fourth day, they knew that the expedition would be a success. After they had set up camp at an abandoned oasis called Iren Dabasu, Walter Granger and two other scientists drove off in one of the trucks to see what they could find. When they returned at sunset, Granger strolled over to Andrews' tent and emptied his pockets.

"Well, Roy, we've done it," he said, holding out a handful of fossils. "The stuff is here. We picked up fifty pounds of bone in an hour."[5]

3
THE MONSTER MAMMAL

Paleontologists today still follow Walter Granger's rule: never dig for bones until you see them.

It's a waste of time and energy to dig at random. First, a paleontologist looks for the right kinds of rock. Fossils are found in sedimentary rocks, such as mudstone, slate, clay, limestone, and sandstone. These rocks are built up as layer upon layer of windblown or waterborne gravel, sand, silt, and clay are stacked up and compressed over millions of years. But paleontologists also look for deposits of sedimentary rocks that have been cut by erosion into gullies, canyons, cliffs, or ravines. When a cross section of the rock layers is exposed by erosion, ends or parts of bones are likely to show.

Not all sedimentary rocks contain fossils. If rock was deposited at a time or place where there was no animal life, or a time not favorable to the preservation of bones, there will be no fossils.

The Gobi Desert turned out to be a great place for fossils because the soil and surface layers are constantly being scoured off the ancient sedimentary rock by winds, snow, and blasting sand. And bones buried quickly under the dry sand in the Gobi are so well preserved that often very tiny details can be seen, sometimes even the grooves and pits where blood vessels and nerves went through the bones. Some bones are still articulated, which means that they are attached at the joints. Where skeletons have been washed away in riverbeds or scattered and chewed by scavenging animals, fossil-hunters may find a skull, a few vertebrae, or perhaps a leg bone. But in the Gobi it is not uncommon to find a skeleton of an entire animal just as it was when it was buried by a sudden sandstorm.

Fossil hunting is not a high-tech business, nor is it a job for impatient people. The essential equipment is a soft brush, rock hammer, chisel, and small picks. Some paleontologists walk slowly in circles, others amble back and forth over an imaginary square or in a loop, but all keep their eyes to the ground, deep in concentration. Suddenly, they'll fall to their knees and begin to brush gently with their dry paintbrushes. Next, they'll pick away at the rock with small dental tools, perhaps for hours, until the bone is finally uncovered.

Andrews said, "I can find fossils right enough, but my impetuous nature is not suited to the delicate operation of removing them. My pickax methods do get quick results, but they are a bit rough on the specimens, I must admit. In the language of the expedition, when a fossil is broken beyond repair, it has been given the R.C.A. treatment."[1]

On all the Central Asiatic Expeditions, the best places for fossils and the finest specimens seemed to be discovered just when the men were getting ready to leave a dig site for other fields. That was certainly true that first summer when they found the Beast of Baluchistan, a monster mammal related to the rhinoceros.

At night around the campfire, the Mongolians had talked about a place where they could find bones the size of a man's body. Andrews and his men assumed these were just tall tales. But one afternoon, Granger and the photographer, J. B. Shackelford, had gone off to an area they called Wild Ass Camp, where they had seen wild donkeys. Shackelford had been following a dry riverbed when he literally stumbled over a huge bone sticking out of the ground. It was the lower bone of the front leg—the ulna— of a mammal known then as *Baluchitherium*. It had been named for Baluchistan, India, where a neck vertebra and a foot bone of this animal had once been found.

A few days later, just before breaking camp, the Chinese driver, Wang, wandered into a gully, where he discovered the upper front leg bone, which really was as big as a man's body. That night Andrews had a vivid dream of finding a skull of this monster in a canyon. The next morning, his dream came true when he saw a chunk of bone poking out of the sand in a gully. He

A Therian mammal, just 5 inches long, is typical
of the fossils that can be found in the Gobi.

yelled for Wang and Shackelford, but he was already on his knees, laughing and digging like a dog when they came running. It was a giant skull.

"Even though we realized that the *Baluchitherium* was a colossal beast," Andrews wrote later, "the size of the bones left us absolutely astounded."[2]

The largest known rhinoceros was dwarfed by comparison. The head of this animal was five feet long. In life it was seventeen feet high at the shoulder, almost twice as tall as the average elephant, and twenty-four feet long. A man could have walked upright under its belly. It was the largest land mammal that ever lived. It was built to browse on leaves from a tree's top branches, but when the climate changed and forests began to disappear, it probably could not get enough to eat and became extinct.

It took four days to dig out the huge skull. After Granger whisked away loose dirt and sand with a fine camel's-hair brush to uncover the bone, he painted it with a glue called gum arabic. Then he stippled soft, tough rice paper into every crack and crevice to keep the bone from shattering. Finally he soaked strips of burlap in flour paste and bandaged the whole thing. When it dried, the wrapping was like a plaster cast on a broken leg, and strong enough to survive the long journey back to New York by way of camel, truck, railroad, and steamship.

Other exciting discoveries turned up on that first expedition, including *Mononykus,* an ancient flightless bird the size of a turkey, with short, stubby arms that ended in a single claw. They also found a mosquito in a thin layer of paper-shale ten or twelve million years old, and a butterfly's wing so well preserved that its delicate veins were visible. The paper-shales are made from thin layers of fine sediments that filter to the bottom of still water. Insects that die on the water's surface sink to the bottom and decay. But their bodies make impressions in the silt, and they are covered by more fine sediments that eventually turn to stone.

Mononykus had a body design similar to the roadrunner. It is more closely related to modern birds than *Archeopteryx* is. The discovery of *Mononykus* was important because it revealed a step in the slow evolution from carnivorous dinosaur to the modern bird.

By the time these treasures had been packed for shipment, summer was almost over. One morning, a light blanket of new snow covered the camp. That was enough to make Andrews decide that nothing but the discovery of the Missing Link itself would keep the expedition from heading home. The cold didn't bother the men in their

Andrews and the skull of a *Baluchitherium,* the largest land mammal that ever lived

fur-lined coats, but snow was a real danger. In midwinter when the ground is frozen solid, light snow is easy to drive over, but in autumn, a snowfall can turn the ground into mud that can trap a car.

On September 1, Andrews and the men in the first car were searching for a small trail they thought would lead to a road. Their water supply was getting low. The last drop had been put into the cars and everyone was thirsty. They had seen no one for at least a hundred miles. When they finally saw a *yurt* (Mongolian dwelling), the line of cars stopped and Andrews ran to ask for water and directions.

A yurt (today called a *ger*) is a round collapsible tent that can be taken down and packed on a camel in less than an hour. Its single wall is an expandable wooden crisscross skeleton like a folding gate. Around this nomads wrap a thick layer of felt made from camel wool, a good insulator. The whole structure is then covered with windproof canvas, with the doorway facing south.

Because nomads have few visitors, it is not polite to rush in, ask a question, and leave. So while Andrews sat on a small stool in the yurt, drinking *airag*

A modern ger under construction (*above*) and finished (*facing page*)

(fermented mare's milk—the national drink) with his Mongol host, some of the men wandered off to look around.

Shackelford found himself on the rim of a huge red basin. Perhaps his training as a photographer made him especially observant, because he immediately spotted a skull. As Andrews described it, "Half way down the steep slope, a white skull, about eight inches long, rested on the summit of a sandstone pinnacle. He picked it off and hurried back. None of us had ever seen its like. Granger was only able to say that it was a new type of reptile, unknown to science."[3]

They named this parrot-beaked dinosaur *Protoceratops andrewsi*, in honor of the expedition's leader. Later they found so many of these hog-sized, plant-eating dinosaurs with a bony frill around the neck that they seemed to have been as common as sheep.

Andrews said that Shackelford's discovery was so important that they knew they had to search further. The Mongol had told him that there was a well on the basin floor, and they decided to camp there for the night, refill their water supply, and look around the next day.

The early Gobi expeditions turned up a number of parrot-beaked *Protoceratops* fossils (*top*). Dr. Walter Granger (*above*) of the American Museum of Natural History is shown readying a *Protoceratops* skeleton for exhibit.

In the setting sun, the red sandstone cliffs looked to Andrews like shooting tongues of fire, and he named them the Flaming Cliffs. The next morning every man explored the basin, buttes, and crevices that had been carved by sandstorms. Against the red sandstone, edges of white bones gleamed in the sunlight. Andrews said that the area was almost paved with bones.

It was hard for them to leave this place, but with snow in the air they were in danger of being trapped in a blizzard. Just before they left, Walter Granger picked up a few broken bits of fossil eggshells, thinking they belonged to an extinct bird. None of them had any idea that these few broken shells would lead them to the most famous eggs in the world.

4

DINOSAUR EGGS

Entry from Roy Chapman Andrews' 1923 field journal:

The Red Beds. We arrived there at 3 pm on July 8th. This was the most important locality of that entire summer's work.

The day as beautiful as anyone could want—brilliant sun, crystal-clear air, and just warm enough to be comfortable without a coat.

All the men scattered over the Cretaceous exposure immediately after breakfast, carrying brushes, small picks, and collecting sacks. We expected to get only teeth and fragments of dinosaur bones for the rather hurried search of last year seemed to indicate that the skeletons had been badly broken up by water action before they were deposited.

The most important discoveries, however, proved to be two nests of dinosaur eggs. It had never been known whether or not dinosaurs laid eggs; none had ever been found. The first nest consisted of five eggs closely laid together like those of a hen; they were only two and a half inches long by two inches wide. Olsen took up the entire block with the entire nest in position.

The second "clutch" included five eggs much larger than the first. They are elliptical and typical of reptile shape about six inches long by two inches wide. The shells are very thin, pebbled and yellowish brown in color. Just above them lay the pelvis and one hind limb of a small clawed dinosaur.[1]

George Olsen was one of the scientists new to the 1923 expedition. He was the one who had wandered into the Flaming Cliffs camp at lunchtime saying, "I found dinosaur eggs." When the men kidded him, he had told them, "Laugh if you want to, but they are eggs all right. Come with me."

At first sight, Andrews thought the dinosaur eggs looked like small, hard sandstone nodules called concretions or maybe bird eggs. In the late Cretaceous period, 85 million to 80 million years ago, when these rock layers were formed, mammals, birds, and dinosaurs were evolving together, although birds were rare. But judging by the shape, size, and crinkled texture of the eggs, the scientists were quite sure they were dinosaur eggs. They also agreed that the eggs probably belonged to *Protoceratops* because these small dinosaurs were so common.

As Olsen continued to scrape away sand and loose rock around the nest, he uncovered parts of a skeleton of a small, clawed dinosaur a few inches from the eggs. From the position of the bones, it looked as though this dinosaur had been buried by a sudden sandstorm just as it was about to rob the eggs from the nest.

In his field journal from the 1923 expedition, Andrews wrote: "The most fragile of Tutankhamen's ['King Tut's'] burial furniture was not handled or packed with greater care than these specimens from the Gobi so many millions of years older than those from that other desert [Egypt] far to the south of us."[2]

The men combed loose wool from the camels and wrapped each fossil in it before it was packed in the wooden crates. After three weeks of collecting at the Flaming Cliffs, they had prepared so many skulls, eggs, and bones for shipping that only half a sack of flour was left. If they used it for food, they would not be able to make the flour paste that strengthened the strips of burlap wrapping. When Andrews asked them what they wanted to do, every man voted to keep the flour for work. Little more than tea was left in their supplies, so they went hunting. Andrews said they didn't even mind eating fried antelope for breakfast, stewed antelope for lunch, and roast antelope for dinner.

When they found that the supply of burlap was almost gone, too, they cut off all the tent flaps. Next they used towels and washcloths, and finally their

The first dinosaur eggs were found on the 1923 expedition,
and their discovery caused worldwide excitement.

clothes. Each man offered something—shirts, underwear, socks, trousers. Many years later, a small dinosaur skull still wrapped in a pair of Roy Chapman Andrews' pajamas was found in a corner of a storage shelf at the American Museum of Natural History.

Andrews was excited about the dinosaur eggs, but he didn't expect the enthusiastic reaction from the public when the expedition returned to the United States. Newspaper reporters swarmed the train at every stop. Several papers and magazines tried to buy exclusive rights to the egg story, but Andrews turned them down. It was everyone's story, he told them. Cartoonists and comic-strip artists had fun with dinosaur eggs, and one New York paper carried a series on dinosaurs for weeks.

Andrews loved it. He said that all this attention made the country more dinosaur-conscious than years of research had. When the eggs were put on display at the museum, people lined up to see them. Some visitors were disappointed because the eggs were so small. Apparently they had pictured an egg at least the size of a football to hold a baby dinosaur.

As a way of gaining publicity and raising money for the next expedition, Andrews decided to auction off one dinosaur egg. Later he regretted it because the idea backfired. Austin Colgate bought the egg for $5,000 and donated it to Colgate University, where it is still on display. But that convinced Mongolian government officials that if one egg was worth $5,000, Andrews was stealing treasures from their country. From then on, they searched the expedition's goods, confiscated fossils, and stalled them with paperwork whenever they could.

Since then, rules for international collecting have been adopted so that any national treasure—whether a dinosaur egg or a jewel from a tomb—belongs to the country where it is found. Now, when paleontologists or archaeologists find specimens, they can take them back to their own country for study. They can make casts and reproductions of them, but the specimens must be returned to museums in their homeland.

Back in the laboratory at the American Museum of Natural History after the 1923 expedition, Dr. Osborn studied the rock-hard eggs and agreed with the scientists on the expedition that they must be from *Protoceratops*. His decision, like theirs, was based on little more than the abundance of these dinosaurs at that site.

Then he examined the small, clawed dinosaur that had been found near the *Protoceratops* eggs, and he agreed that it probably had been suffocated by a sandstorm just as it was robbing the nest. Osborn gave that ostrich-size

Packing the fossils for the long trip to
the American Museum of Natural History

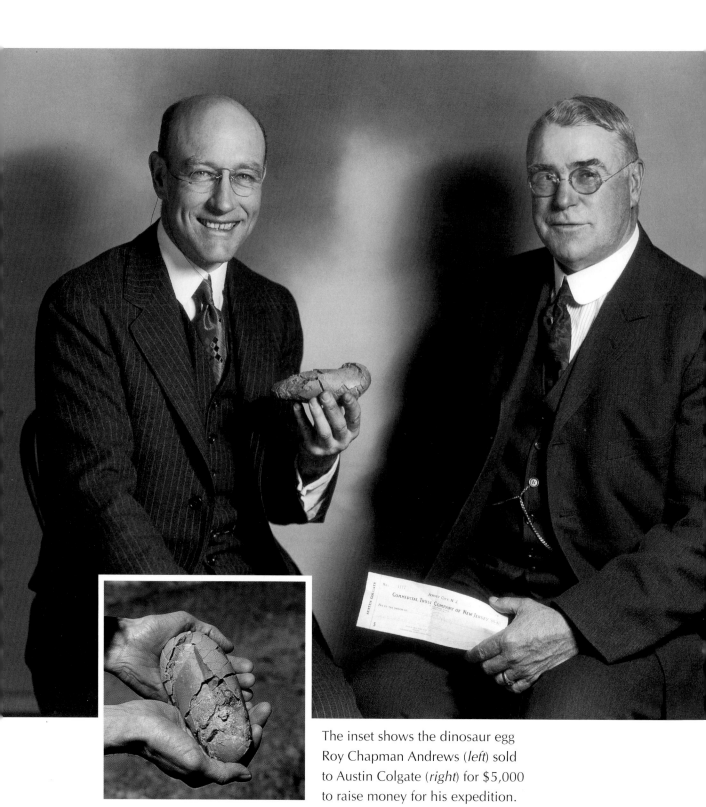

The inset shows the dinosaur egg
Roy Chapman Andrews (*left*) sold
to Austin Colgate (*right*) for $5,000
to raise money for his expedition.

dinosaur the scientific name *Oviraptor philoceratops*. *Ovi* means "egg," *raptor* means "robber," and *philoceratops* means "a fondness for ceratopsian eggs."

It was a mistake that wouldn't be known for more than seventy years.

Another member of the 1923 expedition, Peter Kaisen, found the skull, jaws, a front claw, a hind foot, and a few finger bones of a small therapod. These animals walk on two legs and have three functional toes. Therapods include animals from *Tyrannosaurus* to hummingbirds. Osborn named this one *Velociraptor,* the swift robber, the dinosaur made famous—and greatly exaggerated—in the book and film *Jurassic Park.* Judging by the dinosaur's big eye sockets, large brain case, foot bones, and sharp teeth, Osborn described it as "an alert, swift-moving carnivorous dinosaur." But not much more would be known about this little dinosaur for decades.

The expedition never did find the Missing Link in human evolution, but it did discover an equally important link. It was just a tiny skull in a lump of sandstone. In the laboratory, where it was separated from its surrounding stone (called matrix), it was found to be a tiny placental mammal, no bigger than a shrew.

Placental mammals were the real "missing links" because they were the primitive ancestors of all mammals, including apes and humans. Their presence in that rock layer meant that mammals had been around for millions of years, and that in the era of dinosaurs, one branch of marsupial mammals had already evolved into placental mammals. Marsupial babies, such as opossums and kangaroos, are born prematurely, and they are nurtured in pouches outside the mother's body. Placental mammals, such as humans and raccoons, deliver mature babies that have been nourished through a placenta inside the mother's body.

This discovery fed the theory that dinosaurs became extinct because tiny mammals ate dinosaur eggs. The fossil beds of the Gobi Desert are still the only places where so many skulls and skeletons of mammals of the late Cretaceous period are found.

Another expedition went out in 1925, but Andrews later admitted it was too large, with fifty men, eight motorcars, and 150 camels. Yet, despite the size, which made moving from camp to camp more difficult, Andrews considered that expedition one of the most successful. They mapped previously unexplored parts of the Gobi, studied climate changes, found more dinosaur eggs, and took home seven skulls and parts of skeletons of tiny mammals from the Mesozoic period that marked the close of the age of dinosaurs

And they finally found some evidence of Old Stone Age cultures—crude

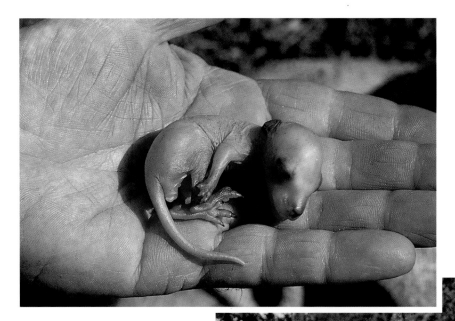

A fossil found on the 1923 expedition proved that at the time of the dinosaurs, marsupial mammals had already evolved into placental mammals. Marsupial babies, such as this nine-week-old wallaby baby (*above*), are born prematurely and must mature in the mother's pouch (*right*).

pottery, drills, and scrapers and arrowheads made from red jasper and slate. Those who made them were not "missing links." They were humans. Andrews called them the Dune Dwellers. When the scientists found bits of dinosaur eggs drilled with neat round holes, probably for a necklace, Andrews said that the Dune Dwellers had really discovered the first dinosaur eggs.

Things weren't always easy for the 1925 expedition. One cold night turned into a nightmare for Andrews. Like Indiana Jones, he hated snakes. That night, the men killed forty-seven poisonous snakes that invaded their tents, nestled in boots, and crawled into sleeping bags trying to get warm.

They were constantly wary of bandits. Andrews said, "Bandits were always a nuisance, but in two or three lively 'incidents' we lost no men." The bandits weren't so lucky. Andrews was never without his pistol, and he was a good shot.

The Russians, who controlled Mongolia at the time, decided that Andrews and his men were spies, so the expedition was held up at almost every town and outpost, sometimes for days, while Andrews negotiated the outrageous fees demanded on each camel, car, and man.

The 1926 expedition was canceled, but Andrews was determined to try again. The 1928 expedition returned to the Flaming Cliffs. This time they found many nests of eggs close together on a sand bank. Andrews said that this sand bank must have been as popular as a bathing beach in summer, because the region literally swarmed with dinosaurs. Although they found the remains of hundreds of these extinct reptiles, they couldn't begin to guess how many others had gathered millions of years ago in similar breeding grounds in the Gobi.

At the close of the 1928 expedition, Chinese government agents confiscated every rock and bone the scientists had collected. Andrews appealed to the U.S. ambassador, and after weeks of negotiation, the expedition finally got its fossils back. But China's Society for the Preservation of Cultural Objects continued to accuse Andrews of stealing treasures, spying, smuggling opium, and searching for oil and minerals.

The 1929 expedition was also canceled. The United States was deep in an economic depression. Millions of people were out of work, and there was no money for exploring. In 1930 political unrest in Asia made it too dangerous for foreigners to work there. Andrews moved out of the house in Peking and returned to the United States.

The era of glorious expeditions for American scientists had come to an end. Mongolia and fossil hunting were forgotten during the years of World

The loaded cars on the 1928 expedition

War II. Decades passed. Perhaps only paleontologists remembered what Andrews had written about the Gobi Desert:

> *Doubtless it will be the hunting ground of other expeditions for years to come. We have but scratched the surface, and every season of blasting gales will expose more riches hidden in its rocks. Who can tell what will come from a place that has given us so much already?*[3]

5
RETURN
TO THE
GOBI

Many things have changed in Mongolia since Roy Chapman Andrews led the Central Asiatic Expeditions more than seventy years ago. After the communist government fell in the Soviet Union in 1990, Mongolia was the first of its satellite nations to declare itself an independent republic. In a free market economy, without the guarantee of work and with few industries, life is a struggle for many Mongolians.

Only 2.2 million people live in Mongolia, less than the population of the city of Baltimore. Most of them are nomads and still live in their traditional gers (*yurt* is a Russian word no longer used). But each year more people move to the capital city, Ulaan Bataar (formerly Urga), where there are Russian-style concrete-slab apartment buildings, new hotels, universities, embassies, government buildings, and a few factories. Now and then a motorcycle roars away from a ger camp, and people use buses and cars in the cities.

Air Mongolia flies passengers and mail to Ulaan Bataar twice a week, and television carries CNN and American cartoons. Tourists are encouraged to stay in ger camps. They visit landmarks in old school buses that jolt and jostle over

A view of modern Ulaan Bataar, Mongolia,
north toward the city center

deeply rutted trails marked with no signs other than an occasional exclamation point, which has no explanation.

But many things have stayed the same. Mongolia is still dotted with herds of sheep, goats, and yaks. There are more horses than people, and camels provide reliable transportation, meat, milk, wool, and dung for fuel. The weather is just as harsh and unpredictable as it has always been. Although railroads now crisscross the country, there are fewer than six hundred miles of paved roads, most of which are around the capital.

The older Mongolians, and sometimes young people on holiday, still wear their colorful, pointed leather boots, and the traditional *del,* a knee-length coat buttoned at the right shoulder and tied with a brightly colored sash.

A Mongolian couple
in native dress

Everyone drinks airag and eats a lot of mutton, but vegetables are scarce because the growing season is too short for farming most crops.

During the years when American scientists did not dig in the Gobi Desert, Mongolian, Russian, and Polish scientists did. Not far from the Flaming Cliffs, the complete skeletons of an amazing pair of dinosaurs locked in battle were excavated by a team of Polish and Mongolian paleontologists in 1971. At the Mongolian Museum of Natural History in Ulaan Bataar, these dinosaurs are on exhibit, in the same position they were in when they were buried by a sudden sandstorm. *Velociraptor* has hold of *Protoceratops* by the snout, and one of its knife-sharp claws on a hind foot is buried in the smaller dinosaur's belly.[1]

In 1990, the Mongolian Academy of Science invited paleontologists from the American Museum of Natural History to return to the Gobi Desert. No invitation could have been received with more joy. Dr. Malcolm McKenna, Dr. Michael Novacek, and Dr. Mark Norell went to Mongolia for two weeks, just long enough to find something to justify funding a longer expedition.

Each of these scientists has a Ph.D. in paleontology and many years of field work in America's western states, South America, and other parts of the world. They grew up reading the books of Roy Chapman Andrews, and they were eager to see the Flaming Cliffs. McKenna said that the first scientific word he ever learned as a boy was *Baluchitherium*.

▾ ▾ ▾ ▾ ▾ ▾

No women took part in any of Andrews' expeditions, but field work has been open to all scientists for many years. Zofia Kielan-Jaworowska was the leader of the Polish team for the 1971 expedition when two other women, Halszka Osmolska and Teresa Maryanska, discovered the fighting *Protoceratops* and *Velociraptor*.

Travel was easier this time. Instead of weeks on a ship, the New York team flew in one day to Beijing (formerly Peking), then took the Trans-Siberian Express train to Ulaan Bataar. While they waited to have paperwork and permission forms signed by Mongolian officials, they stayed in the comfortable Bayongol Hotel.

Dr. Demberelyin Dashzeveg, a Mongolian paleontologist with more than thirty years experience in the Gobi, guided the U.S. scientists to the desert. Using Russian GAZ trucks didn't guarantee any smoother ride for the 1990 group than Andrews' men had in the 1920s cars. Novacek said that they

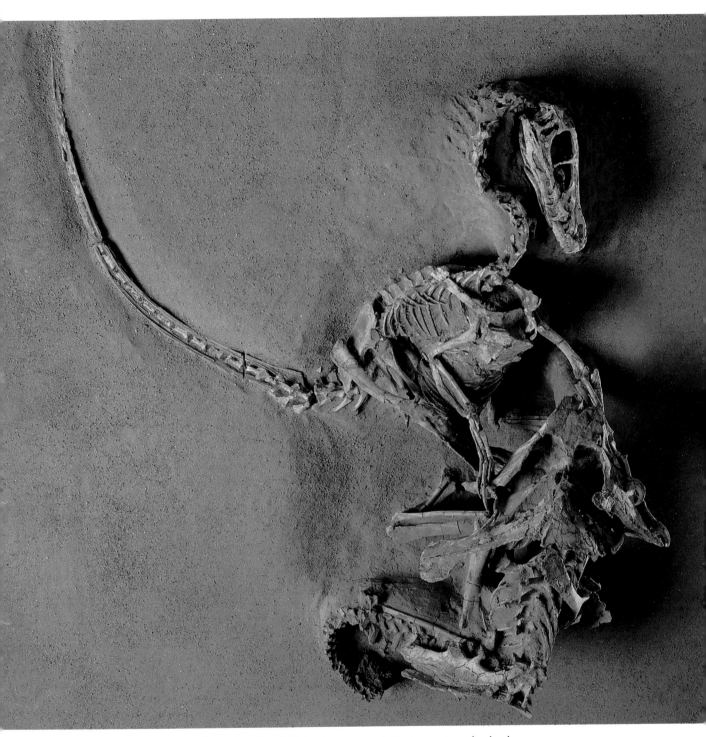

These fossils of *Velociraptor* and *Protoceratops* locked
in a struggle to the death were found in 1971.

bounced over washboard roads like a canoe in a cataract. Blowing sand fouled engines and damaged transmissions. Once a Mongolian driver had to repair a gasket with a cardboard disk cut from an oatmeal box.

When the 1990 team camped in the desert, it might have been 1923. The air was as crystal-clear as Andrews described it, and the heat as overwhelming. The barren desert was silent, and hawks and vultures circled in the brilliant blue sky as they had in the days of Kublai Khan.

In Andrews' camps, the men had cots in their tents and cooks served meals on tablecloths. Today's campsites are a cluster of small, yellow, dome tents with room enough for sleeping bags. Scattered among the tents and trucks are canvas safari chairs, aluminum food lockers, and a solar generator for recharging batteries for cameras, laptop computers, and walkie-talkies.

Even the scientists have a different look—T-shirts, cutoffs, baseball caps, sunglasses, sandals, scruffy beards and long hair, in contrast to the 1920s' high boots, jodphers, wide-brimmed felt hats, and every man in matching sweaters for group photos.

In their brief visit, McKenna, Novacek, and Norell gathered dinosaur eggs, a *Protoceratops* skull, and a complete skeleton of an ankylosaurus, a stubby-legged dinosaur with an armored body and a club at the end of its tail. But they hoped to find something really spectacular, something new. And that happened when they dug up an eight-inch-long skull of a lizard that had never been known before. They named it *Estesia mongoliensis.* It is similar to the Komodo dragons of Indonesia, but the canals at the base of *Estesia's* knife-edged teeth suggest that it may have injected poison into its victims as a Gila monster does. That discovery alone was more than enough to warrant more exploration of the Gobi. Before they returned to the United States, they negotiated an agreement with the Mongolian Academy of Sciences for three full-scale expeditions.

The 1991 expedition lasted all summer. Added to the team of Novacek, Norell, McKenna, and Dashzeveg were another Mongolian scientist, Altangerlin Perle and his son Chimbald, Dr. McKenna's wife, Priscilla, and paleontologists Lowell Dingus and James Clark.

Priscilla McKenna, who had accompanied her husband on many expeditions, was in charge of Magellan, a portable instrument that is part computer, part radio receiver. It links to American satellites in the Global Positioning System (GPS). When it picks up signals from at least three satellites, it can calculate the longitude, latitude, and elevation of the receiver, and compute the distance and direction to a destination. While this equipment doesn't guaran-

Dr. Mark Norell really gets close to his work
on his 1991 expedition to the Gobi.

Modern instruments make position checks easy. Dr. Malcolm McKenna
is using an instrument that links to the satellite Global Positioning System.

tee that users won't get lost in a dead-end pass through sand dunes or gullies, it does head them in the right direction and tell them where they've been so they can return. Mapmaking is much easier with the GPS.[2]

This time they drove four-wheel drive Mitsubishi Monteros purchased in southern California, where the vehicles had been customized for driving over sand dunes. They had all the extras—air-conditioning, stereo tape decks, and roof racks. But those luxuries didn't matter much when there was no fuel.

Gas and food were still in short supply in Mongolia. The expedition had planned on buying fresh bread and vegetables to add to their freeze-dried dinners and tins of tuna and sardines, but store shelves in Ulaan Bataar and outpost towns were empty. Lunch for the expedition was often reduced to a sardine or two and a foil-wrapped fruit bar. Everyone was hungry and their energy was low, especially in the heat. Days of endless wind blew sand into tents, cars, food, and clothing. Even though they wore sun goggles, sand filtered into their eyes, causing irritation and swelling. And when the wind dropped, camel ticks and flies swarmed over them. But they kept going.

Like Andrews' expeditions, they often made some of their best finds late in the afternoon on the last day. Their most exciting find was the skull and lower jaw of a *Velociraptor,* lying only partly buried in the sand like a seashell on a beach. They also found a perfect skull of a small placental mammal called *Zalambdalestes,* which may turn out to be the ancestor of rabbits, and the skulls of many other small mammals. But still they wondered if they would ever live up to the reputation of the Central Asiatic Expeditions.

They certainly didn't want to give up. Bones found in the Gobi Desert are extraordinary, but often they don't reveal their secrets right away. Paleontologists follow a rule: never prepare a fossil in the field. That means they wait until they get back to the lab before they chip and cut the fossil from its surrounding rock and examine it carefully.

In the field, they "jacket" the bone as Andrews' team did, but now they coat it first with Butvar, a plastic powder mixed with acetone, instead of glue or gum arabic. And instead of rice paper, they use a layer of toilet paper as a separator between the bone and the next layer of plaster bandages. Instead of burlap or cloth strips dipped in flour and water, they use plaster-embedded gauze, the kind of "instant casts" doctors use.

When the cast has dried and the exposed part of the bone is secure in this covering, they cut it away from its rock base, turn it over, and jacket the underside. Only then will the fossil be protected well enough to pack in foam rubber for shipping. At the museum lab, a preparator may spend hundreds of hours cutting a bone from its jacket and cleaning it for study.

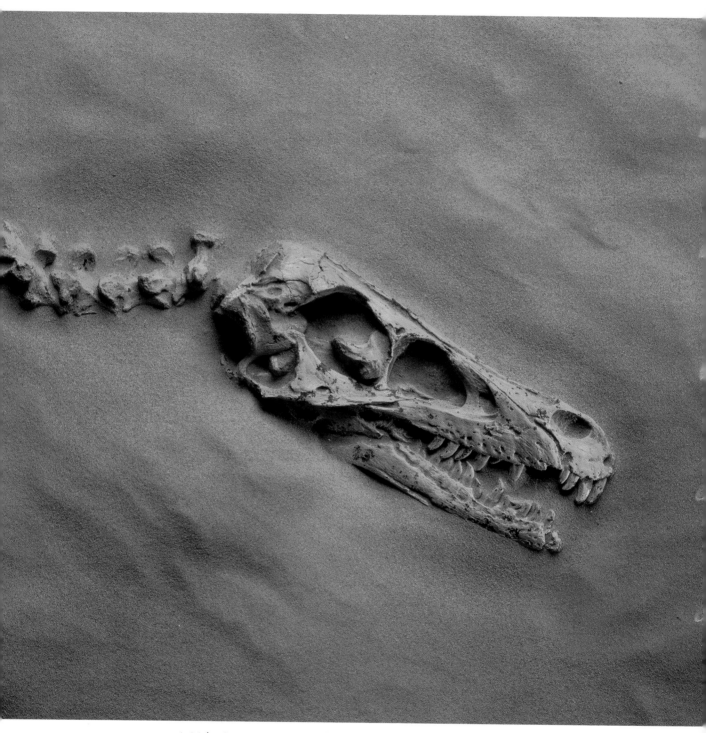

A *Velociraptor* is not very large as dinosaurs go, but its skull,
shown here, is seven times the size of the 1-inch skull of a
Zalambdalestes, a small placental mammal found in the Gobi in 1991.

In the field, paleontologists can read the exposed ridges and hollows on a bone. From years of study and practice they can recognize a jaw bone of a mammal or a tooth of a reptile. They can tell a carnivore by its knife-sharp teeth, and the difference between a plant-eater that browsed and one that grazed. They can judge the size of a dinosaur by measuring its stride—the length between its footprints. The arrangement of footprints tells them whether the animal traveled alone or in herds, and whether young animals traveled with adults. A mixed stride of long then short steps might mean an injured animal limped, and tell whether or not it kept up with the others. A thick ridge on a bone shows where massive muscles were attached. Heavy muscles at the top and bottom of a tail bone are evidence that the dinosaur could balance its tail straight out when it walked. There are clues in the size and position of a dinosaur's eye sockets or the size of its brain case.

But identifications made in the field are sometimes educated guesses, and paleontologists know that lab work will reveal much more. Today's scientists can turn to techniques and equipment that Granger and Andrews could not have imagined.

An electron microscope can enlarge a bone cell hundreds of times more than conventional microscopes used in the 1920s. Under ultraviolet lights, fossil bones glow against their rock matrix, making them easier to work on. Without breaking open a skull, a scientist can now examine it with a CAT scan (computerized axial tomography), a machine that takes cross-sectional X rays at intervals as small as a half-millimeter. When these "slices" are put together, they create a three-dimensional image that can be seen on a monitor. For example, the part of the brain called the cerebrum processes vision. If that area of the dinosaur's skull is well developed and shows evidence of a rich blood supply, it suggests the animal could see well and that it probably was a good hunter. If the olfactory center was developed, the animal might have been a scavenger that needs a good sense of smell.

◄

The 1992 expedition got off to a bad start. It was big—too big, Novacek said later—with eight vehicles and twenty-five people, including an expert mechanic and a production crew from BBC-TV. Mongolia was in worse shape economically than it had been in 1991. Gas and food were still scarce, and the expedition's supplies and equipment were held up for weeks at the Mongolia-China border.

But at a site called Tugrugeen, not far from the Flaming Cliffs, Jim Clark

It takes many hours of painstaking laboratory work to remove
fossils from their protective coating and surrounding material.

and Mark Norell uncovered the skull of a *Velociraptor* with holes in the top of
the skull that went clean through into the brain cavity. The holes matched the
spacing and size of teeth in the upper jaw of other *Velociraptors*. Evidence like
this is as exciting to a paleontologist as a fingerprint on a gun is to a detective
because it is a clue to the behavior of these animals. Were *Velociraptors* canni-
bals? Were the two animals fighting over a mate or territory? This skull was
more complete than others they had found, and they know that further study
of it will tell them more about *Velociraptor's* "higher" intelligence and its sim-
ilarity to birds.

They also picked up a lot of small mammal skulls encased in concretions that eroded out of the cliffs. But they passed up some big dinosaurs, marking them for another year. They weren't ignoring the huge beasts, but there was no hurry because many of these had been collected and studied in the past. The goal of this expedition was to find another "red bed," equal to the Flaming Cliffs in its store of new species.

And then, Jim Clark made a discovery that had nothing to do with dinosaurs. In an area about as big as a backyard wading pool, he found the parts and shells of fifty fossil turtles. A find like this stretches the imagination to "see" this dead, dry desert as it might have been 75 million years ago, teeming with life in and around the ponds of an oasis.[3]

A find like this was fascinating enough to make the paleontologists forget the hunger, thirst, flies, and other miseries, and begin to plan the next year's work in the Gobi.

6

OVIRAPTOR'S SECRET

Xanadu, the Golden City, the summer palace of the infamous Kublai Khan, was the name the American team gave to the eroded cliffs and spires at Ukhaa Tolgod, the "brown hills" where they found the world's greatest treasure of ancient animals in 1993. Michael Novacek described this dry basin among the hills as peppered with complete skeletons of 80-million-year-old dinosaurs, mammals, and lizards from the late Cretaceous.

But they almost missed it. Three years before, they had turned away from these hills to explore other canyons and cliffs.

The books of Roy Chapman Andrews are dramatic in their descriptions of the Flaming Cliffs and other fossil-rich sites, but Michael Novacek's passion for paleontology is no less evident in his book *Dinosaurs of the Flaming Cliffs.* Writing about that first day at the Ukhaa Tolgod site, Xanadu, Novacek said,

> *A strange feeling started to take hold in me. At first it was only a twinge, a rush that made me shiver every time I saw yet another mammal skull or dinosaur skeletons sculpted in the rock. . . . I had the growing realization that I was having a day like no other in twenty years of field prospecting.*

Mark [Norell] felt the same excitement, though we were both too superstitious to say anything. Like Granger and Andrews when they discovered their first nest of dinosaur eggs at Flaming Cliffs, we couldn't believe that our encounter with this fossil-laden patch of ground was real.[1]

In an area no bigger than a football field, they had found treasures that matched all the riches of other famous Gobi sites put together. By lunchtime that first day, Novacek had found twenty-two skulls, including thirteen mammals, which was more than Granger and other members of the 1925 expedition had found in a week. Combined with Norell's collection, they had found sixty dinosaur, mammal, and lizard skulls in three hours!

This time, the expedition had taken no chances of being held back by a gas shortage. A tanker truck carrying 1,300 gallons of gas for the Russian GAZ trucks towed a tank trailer full of 780 gallons of higher-octane gas for the Mitsubishis. But it was a struggle to get these huge vehicles over sand dunes and across gullies as they headed west, away from the Flaming Cliffs. When it took seven hours to drive thirty miles, Novacek realized why Ukhaa Tolgod had not been explored. Andrews never could have made it through this rough terrain with his touring cars.

The 1993 expedition was limited to a small group of professionals with years of field experience. There were no journalists, photographers, or visitors. McKenna and his wife, Priscilla, were working in another area, with plans to join the main expedition later. So the team consisted of Novacek, Norell, Clark, Dashzeveg, a paleontologist from Argentina, Luis Chiappe, and Amy Davidson, a sculptor and preparator at the American Museum of Natural History. She was skilled at the tedious detail work of taking the fossils from their jackets and matrices and getting them ready for study or exhibit.

After lunch that first day, Mark Norell found a concentration of dinosaur eggs and nests. Among fragments of shells and eggs in one group, he saw one egg that had broken open, revealing the tiny bones of an embryo dinosaur. The seven-inch-long egg was oval shaped, and its surface was crinkled—the same kind of egg George Olsen had found at the Flaming Cliffs seventy years before. These were just like the eggs from the dinosaur named *Protoceratops*. But no one had ever seen an embryo in one of those eggs. They were solid rock. Even though this team recognized a few bones in the egg as those of a carnivore, the identification would have to wait until Amy Davidson went to work on this embryo in the lab.

As Norell kept brushing and picking in that same nest, he found two small

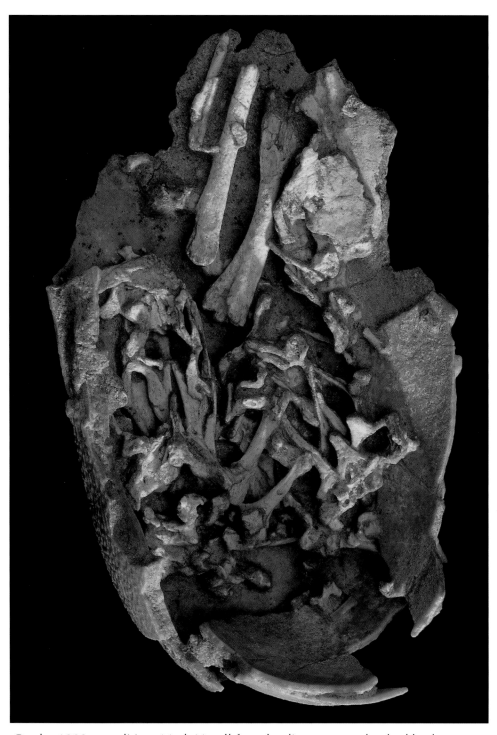

On the 1993 expedition, Mark Norell found a dinosaur egg that had broken open before it was fossilized, revealing the first dinosaur embryo ever discovered.

skulls of a sharp-toothed, meat-eating dinosaur. These were the first carnivore hatchlings they'd ever seen. But why were they in this nest? That answer would also have to wait for lab work.

At the end of that first day they had found seventy-five mammal and lizard skulls and skeletons, more than forty dinosaurs marked for jacketing, and the eggs, embryos, and hatchlings. But the digging would only get better!

In one spot, which Novacek described as no bigger than a putting green, he found seven ankylosaur skeletons. Norell found a headless skeleton that seemed to be an *Oviraptor,* which would take several days to jacket and haul out. And then Novacek found a delicate skull of a small carnivorous dinosaur they had never seen before. Its huge forward-pointing eyes and large brain case suggested that this might turn out to be one of the "smartest" dinosaurs.

Every member of the team was busy brushing, picking, and jacketing new specimens. Each new find seemed more exciting than the last, but one discovery sent a shock through the camp. Luis Chiappe and Amy Davidson were chipping away at an *Oviraptor* skeleton when they found eggs under it. They knew immediately that it was a major scientific discovery, but they had to wait until they could examine it in the lab before they made an announcement. It could not have been easy to resist more probing around the skeleton to get a better look at the eggs. But they wrapped the entire skeleton and eggs in plaster and hoisted the six-hundred-pound mass into the truck.

During the winter of 1993–1994, Davidson spent more than four hundred hours cleaning the bones of the tiny embryo in its eggshell. The seventy-year-old mistake was finally corrected. The embryo was not *Protoceratops,* but an *Oviraptor.* The *Oviraptor* found in 1923 at the Flaming Cliffs was not an egg robber. She was probably protecting her own nest.

The small skulls of the two other carnivores in the nest were identified as very young *Velociraptors.* But why were they in this nest? There are several possibilities. The eggs of those hatchlings could have been dropped into the nest for the *Oviraptor* mother to incu-

> ▹ ▹ ▹ ▹ ▹ ▹
>
> Scientific names follow rules set by the International Code of Zoological Nomenclature (ICZN). The first person to describe a new species gets to choose the name. *Oviraptor*'s name will not change because of the rules. *Brontosaurus,* however, had its name changed to *Apatosaurus* after it was discovered that they were the same dinosaur, and *Apatosaurus* had been discovered first.

It takes a lot of effort to move 600 pounds of dinosaur fossils encased in plaster.

bate and raise, the way a cuckoo bird puts its eggs into the nest of other birds. Or they could be the leftover bones from dinner the mother *Oviraptor* carried to her hatchlings, the way a hawk brings a freshly killed mouse to its young. It could even be that the tiny *Velociraptors* were raiding the nest.

Most scientists favor the theory of the young *Velociraptors* as baby-food, because animals like the cuckoo that parasitize another animal's nest are rare, and young carnivores attacking the nest would probably be killed by the mother *Oviraptor*. But the questions may never be answered, unless another expedition turns up more evidence.

When the huge jacket was chipped away from the *Oviraptor* on her nest, they found two layers of eggs in a circle, with the narrow end of each egg pointing out. The mother *Oviraptor* was crouched over the nest, her legs tucked under her body and her long arms with their three-fingered hands and sharp talons curled around the edge of the nest like a big, broody hen.

Since 1923, scientists have known that dinosaurs layed eggs, but they didn't know what happened next. Were dinosaurs like other reptiles that lay eggs and leave them to hatch unattended? This discovery was proof that *Oviraptor* stayed close to her nest, turned the eggs, fed the hatchlings, and even stayed with them in the face of a killer sandstorm that surely choked and buried them.

Anyone who doubts that an animal would stay with its young in the face of a sandstorm has only to think of the emperor penguins of the Antarctic. In their enormous breeding colonies of thousands of birds, each one stands guard over its single egg through horrendous blizzards.

The news of *Oviraptor's* nest made headlines: SCIENTISTS CRACK SECRET ABOUT DINOSAUR EGGS and PARENTHOOD, DINO-STYLE. But why is this considered a major scientific discovery?

Norell said, "It was like finding a snapshot of what the world was like 80 million years ago. Now we know that this nesting behavior actually predates birds."[2]

In his report in the scientific journal *Nature,* Norell wrote, "We don't know if dinosaurs used this posture to control the temperature of the eggs, to shade them from the sun, or to protect the nest from predators."[3]

But this is one of those famous "missing links," another piece of information that shows how closely related birds and dinosaurs are. Most scientists agree that not all dinosaurs are extinct. Some have become birds. The relationship can be seen in their similar bone structure—the brain cavity, the feet with large, forward-pointing toes, the wrist and arm bones similar to a bird's wing, and the S-shaped neck vertebrae.

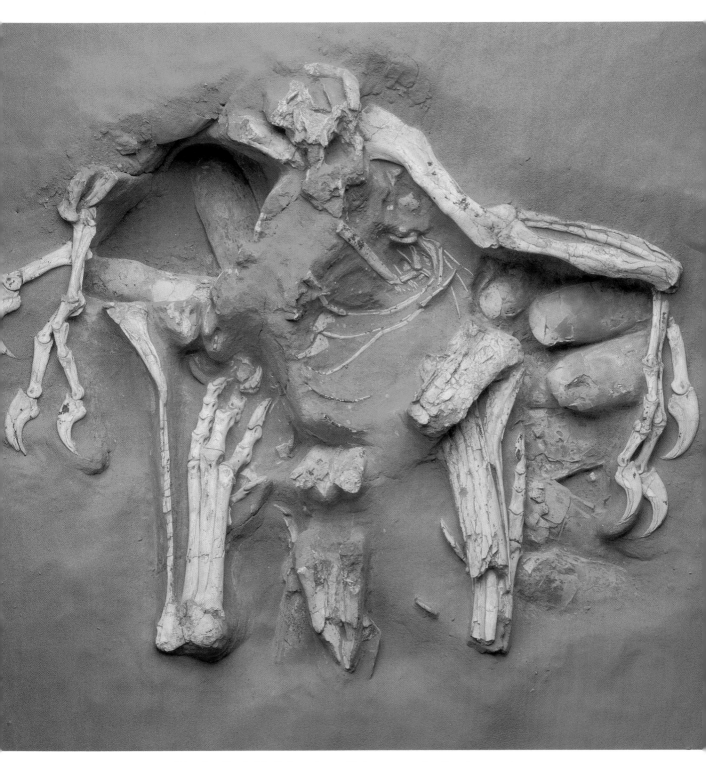

The fossil of this 8-foot-long *Oviraptor* protecting her nest
proved that some dinosaurs were nurturing mothers.

Dinosaur tracks—a path to the past

But the broody *Oviraptor* on her nest is the first direct evidence of dinosaur behavior. We'll probably never know what color dinosaurs were or what noises they made, but in the well-preserved Gobi dinosaurs, there may be more clues to how they lived.

At the American Museum of Natural History in New York City, you can see *Oviraptor* crouched over her nest, just as she died in a wild sandstorm in the Gobi Desert.

Expeditions are finding new dinosaurs all the time—older ones, bigger ones, tinier ones. Different kinds of dinosaur eggs have been found at almost two hundred sites around the world—so many, in fact, that three thousand eggs were confiscated just from people trying to smuggle them out of China in 1993.

But if the ghost of Roy Chapman Andrews ever stalks the dinosaur halls of the American Museum of Natural History, imagine what he must think.

The adventure goes on. The age of discovery is not over.

GLOSSARY

airag: a beverage made from fermented mare's milk; the national drink of Mongolia. Also called koumiss or kumyss.

Cretaceous: the time span between 150 million and 50 million years ago, the last years of the dinosaurs, when birds were evolving.

del: the national costume of Mongolia.

era: a major division of geologic time, made up of several periods.

fossil: the mark or remains of a plant or animal that existed thousands or millions of years ago.

Jurassic: the middle period of the Mesozoic era, when dinosaurs were the dominant animals on earth.

matrix: the rock surrounding a fossil.

Mesozoic: the era of geologic time from 250 million to 50 million years ago, made up of the Triassic, Jurassic, and Cretaceous periods.

paleontologist: a person who studies fossils of the plants and animals that existed in geologic time.

raptor: an animal that preys upon other animals; stealer or robber.

reconnaissance: a general survey or search.

sedimentary rock: rock formed from mud, sand, or other sediments pressed into layers over a long period of time. Most fossils are found in sedimentary rock.

therapod: a bipedal (two-legged) upright dinosaur, such as *Velociraptor,* kin to modern birds. All therapods were meat eaters.

Ulaan Bataar: the capital city of Mongolia, spelled various ways on maps of Mongolia, including Ulan Bator, Ulan Baataar, and Ulaanbataar.

yurt: a round, felt-covered collapsible dwelling, today called a ger or gher, used by nomads in Mongolia.

SOURCE NOTES

Chapter 1

1. Roy Chapman Andrews, *Under a Lucky Star* (New York: Viking Press, 1943), 14.

2. Ibid., 22.

3. Ibid., 24.

4. Ibid., 25.

5. Ibid., 27.

6. Ibid., 35.

7. Ibid., 52.

8. Roy Chapman Andrews, *On The Trail of Ancient Man* (New York: Putnam, 1926), 171.

9. Roy Chapman Andrews, *Ends of the Earth* (New York: Putnam, 1929), 219.

Chapter 2

1. Roy Chapman Andrews, field journal entry (Library, American Museum of Natural History, New York,1923).

2. Andrews, *On The Trail of Ancient Man,* 21.

3. Ibid., 20.

4. Andrews, field journal entry.

5. Andrews, *On The Trail of Ancient Man,* 78.

Chapter 3

1. Roy Chapman Andrews, "The Mongolian Colossus," *Saturday Evening Post,* December 28, 1928.

2. Andrews, *Under a Lucky Star,* 195.

3. Andrews, *On the Trail of Ancient Man,* 180.

Chapter 4

1. Roy Chapman Andrews, field journal entry, 1923.

2. Ibid.

3. Andrews, *On The Trail of Ancient Man,* 340.

Chapter 5

1. Author's journal of Gobi trip, 1995.

2. John Noble Wilford, "Gobi Diary," *New York Times Magazine,* November, 10, 1991, 50–60.

3. Donavan Webster, "Dinosaurs of the Gobi," *National Geographic,* July 1996, 70–89

Chapter 6

1. Michael Novacek, *Dinosaurs of the Flaming Cliffs* (New York: Doubleday, Anchor Books, 1996), 232.

2. Mark Jaffe, "Scientists Crack Secret About Dinosaur Eggs," *Buffalo Evening News,* December 21, 1995.

3. Ibid.

4. Michael Lemonick, "Parenthood, Dino-Style," *Time,* January 8, 1996, 62.

FURTHER READING

Dingus, Lowell, and Mark A. Norell. *Searching for Velociraptor.* New York: HarperCollins, 1996.

Goldensohn, E. (ed.). *Natural History,* vol. 104, no. 6, 1995, 1–88.

Lessem, Don. *Raptors.* Boston: Little, Brown, 1996.

Norell, Mark, Eugene S. Gaffney, and Lowell Dingus. *Discovering Dinosaurs.* New York: Knopf, 1985.

Novacek, Michael. *Dinosaurs of the Flaming Cliffs.* New York: Anchor Books, 1996.

Preston, Douglas J. *Dinosaurs in the Attic.* New York: St. Martin's Press, 1994.

Wallace, Joseph. *The American Museum of Natural History's Book of Dinosaurs and Other Ancient Creatures.* New York: Simon and Schuster, 1994.

Webster, Donovan. "Dinosaurs of the Gobi." *National Geographic,* vol. 190, no. 1, July 1996, 70–89.

Wilford, John Nobel. *The Riddle of the Dinosaur.* New York: Knopf, 1985.

INDEX

ABOUT THE AUTHOR

Margery Facklam is an award-winning author of a number of nonfiction books for young people, including the four-volume *Invaders* series for Twenty-First Century Books, which she wrote with her husband, Howard. She has a bachelor's degree in biology and a master's degree in science education. During the years their five children were in college, she was assistant administrator of education at the Buffalo Museum of Science, curator of education at the Aquarium of Niagara Falls, and coordinator of education at the Buffalo Zoo.

Margery and Howard Facklam live in Clarence Center, New York.